The Nation's #1 Educational Publisher

The McGraw-Hill Companies

Grade 1

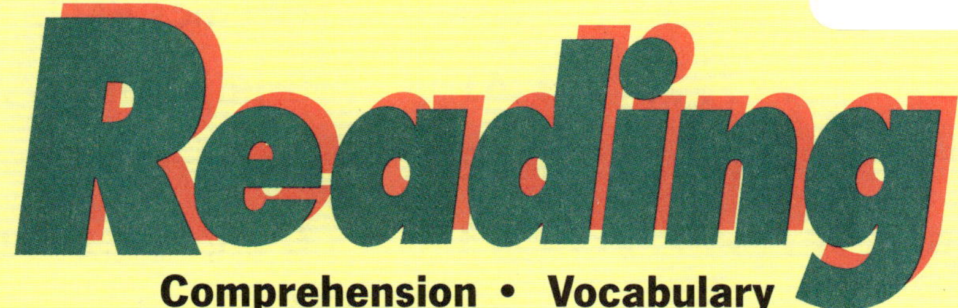

Writing • Phonics

A McGraw-Hill/Warner Bros. Workbook

Table of Contents

Table of Contents (continued)

Credits:
McGraw-Hill Learning Materials Editorial/Production Team
Vincent F. Douglas, B.S. and M. Ed.
Tracy R. Paulus
Jennifer P. Blashkiw

Design Studio
Mike Legendre; Creativity On Demand

Warner Bros. Worldwide Publishing Editorial/Production Team
Michael Harkavy
Charles Carney
Paula Allen
Allen Helbig
Victoria Selover
Sara Hunter

Illustrators
Cover and Interior: Animated Arts!™

McGraw-Hill
Consumer Products
A Division of The ***McGraw-Hill*** *Companies*

Published by McGraw-Hill Learning Materials, an imprint of McGraw-Hill Consumer Products.

Send all inquiries to:
McGraw-Hill Consumer Products
250 Old Wilson Bridge Road
Worthington, Ohio 43085

1-57768-211-4

COMPREHENSION

Boys can fish.
Girls can fish.
Boys and girls can jump.
Can you fish now?

Read the sentence.
Circle the picture that goes with the sentence.

1. The girls can fish.

2. Now the boy can fish.

3. The boys can jump.

4. The girl can jump.

Name

Comprehension

jump   can   fish   now   you

Look at the picture. Choose the right word to finish the sentence. Write the word.

1. The girls fish.

2. Can __________ fish?

3. __________ you can.

4. You __________ jump.

5. The boys __________.

Draw a line under the answer.
Write the word.

1. The boy can ____.
   fish   jump

2. Now ____ can fish.
   boys   you

3. The boy and girl ____.
   jump   run

4. ____ you can jump.
   Now   Can

COMPREHENSION

Read the story. Draw a line under the sentences that tell about the story.

A. The boys jump up and down.
The girls like to jump.
The girls see the boys.
Now the girls can jump.

1. The boys jump.
2. The man can jump.
3. The girls see the boys.
4. The girls can jump.

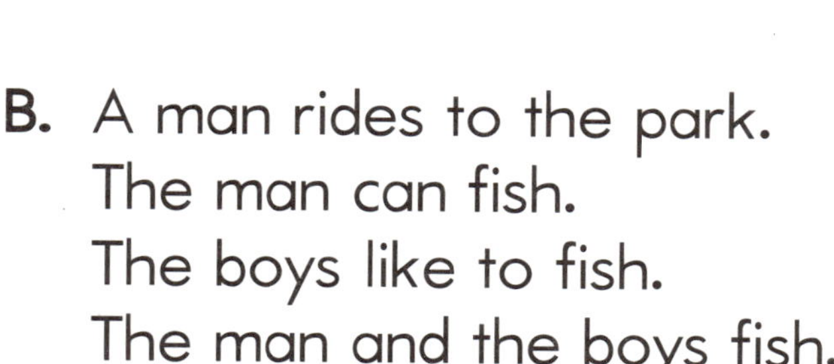

B. A man rides to the park.
The man can fish.
The boys like to fish.
The man and the boys fish.

1. The man rides.
2. The man likes to fish.
3. The girls fish.
4. The boys fish.

PHONICS SKILLS

man

bed

girl

house

Name the picture. Circle the letter with the same **beginning** sound.

1.	2.	3.	4.
h g b m	g h m b	m b g h	b m h g
5.	**6.**	**7.**	**8.**
b m h g	m b g h	h g b m	g h m b
9.	**10.**	**11.**	**12.**
g h m b	h g b m	b m h g	m b g h
13.	**14.**	**15.**	**16.**
h g b m	g h m b	m b g h	b m h g

PHONICS SKILLS

Write the letter. Circle the picture with the same **middle** sound.

1. 

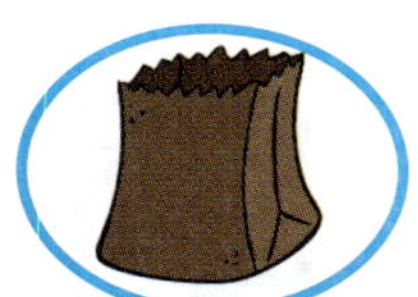

2. 

3. h t

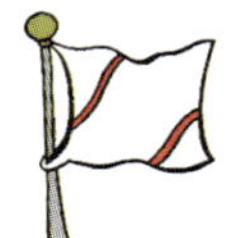

4. 

5. 

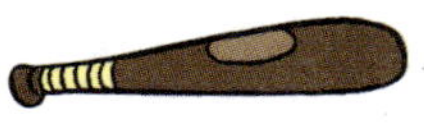

Study Skills

Can You See? by Nat Red	Up and Down by Jan Hut	The Park by Nan Tag

Draw a line from the title of the book to the correct author.

1. Up and Down	Nat Red
2. The Park	Jan Hut
3. Can You See?	Nan Tag

Contents

You See the Fish 3
You See the Man 9
See the Park 13
See the Girls Jump 18

Circle the page number.

1. You See the Man
   3 9 13
2. See the Girls Jump
   9 13 18
3. You See the Fish
   3 13 18
4. See the Park
   3 9 13

COMPREHENSION

She can fish.
Can the boys fish?
Can I?
Now I can fish, too.

Read the sentence.
Circle the picture that goes with the sentence.

1. She can fish.

2. The girls fish.

3. I like to fish.

4. I like to jump, too.

COMPREHENSION

she	I	too	ride

Look at the picture. Choose the right word to finish the sentence. Write the word.

1. I can ride.

2. Can ______ ride?

3. ______ can fish.

4. He can ______.

COMPREHENSION

Draw a line under the answer. Write the word.

1. He can see and ____.
   ride   jump

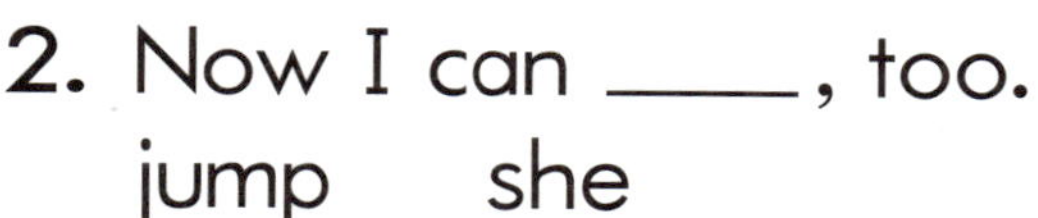

2. Now I can ____, too.
   jump   she

3. I see a ____.
   man   you

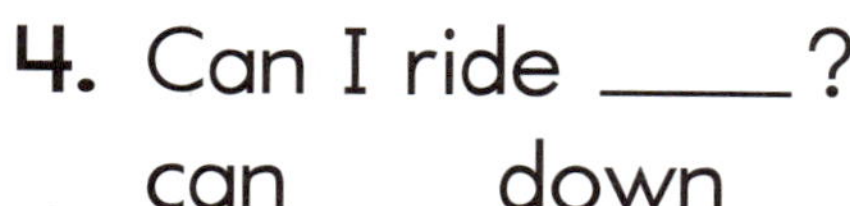

4. Can I ride ____?
   can   down

5. I ____ ride down.
   can   see

6. Now I can ride and ____.
   ride   see

COMPREHENSION

Which sentence tells about the picture?
Fill in the circle.

1. 

ⓐ I like the man.
ⓑ I like to ride.
ⓒ I like to fish.

2. 

ⓐ Can you see the boys?
ⓑ Can you see the fish?
ⓒ Can you see the girls?

3. 

ⓐ The boys ride to the park.
ⓑ The man rides to the park.
ⓒ The girls ride to the park.

4. 

ⓐ He can jump.
ⓑ The boys jump.
ⓒ He can fish.

PHONICS SKILLS

Write the letter. Circle the pictures with the same **ending** sound.

1. 

2. 

3. 

4. 

  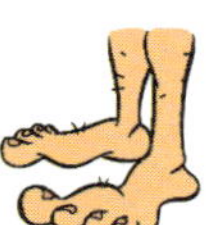

5. 

PHONICS SKILLS

		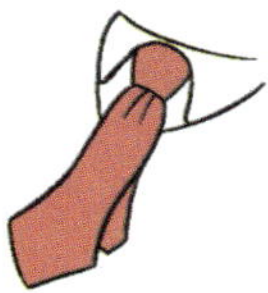	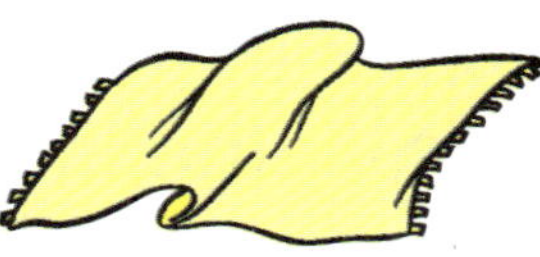
coat	jar	tie	rug

Name the picture. Circle the letter with the same **beginning** sound.

1.  c j t r	2.  j t r c	3.  c j r t	4.  t r c j
5.  j t r c	6.  c j t r	7. 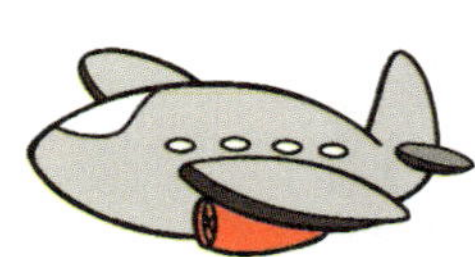 t r c j	8. 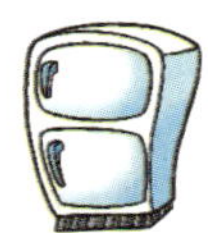 c j r t
9.  c j t r	10.  c j r t	11.  j t r c	12.  t r c j
13.  c j r t	14.  j t r c	15. t r c j	16.  c j t r

PHONICS SKILLS

Read the words. Look at the picture.
Write the right word.

1. **ride**
   rides

A man 

.

2. **ride**
   rides

Girls ______________, too.

3. **like**
   likes

Girls ______________ to fish.

4. **see**
   sees

The girls ______________ a fish.

5. **jump**
   jumps

The fish ______________ up.

Comprehension

Can you see the house?
You like that house.
Can you go in?
You can, but I can't.

Finish the sentence. Draw a line under the word.

1. See ____ man.
   You   that

2. He ____ ride.
   can't   can

3. I ride, ____ he can't.
   jump   but

4. Can you see a ____?
   fish   treehouse

5. I ride to the ____.
   house   fish

6. I can ____ in.
   like   go

Comprehension

but can't go house that

Look at the picture. Choose the word to finish the sentence. Write the word.

1. He can see a house.

2. Can he ______ to the house?

3. He ______ go.

4. Can he jump to ______ house?

5. He can't jump, ______ he can ride.

COMPREHENSION

Which sentence tells about the picture?
Fill in the circle.

1. 

ⓐ Jump on and off.
ⓑ Jump on.

2. 

ⓐ You can go, too.
ⓑ The man can go, too.

3. 

ⓐ Can the mice ride?
ⓑ Can he and I ride?

4. 

ⓐ The boys can't go.
ⓑ You can't go.

5. 

ⓐ I can go now.
ⓑ I can't go.

PHONICS SKILLS

lamp	nest	sock	dog

Name the picture. Circle the letter with the same **beginning** sound.

1. l n s d	2. n l d s	3. s d l n	4. d s n l
5. n l d s	6. s d l n	7. l n s d	8. d s n l
9. s d l n	10. l n s d	11. d s n l	12. n l d s
13. d s n l	14. s d l n	15. n l d s	16. l n s d

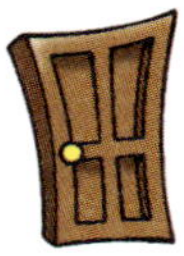

  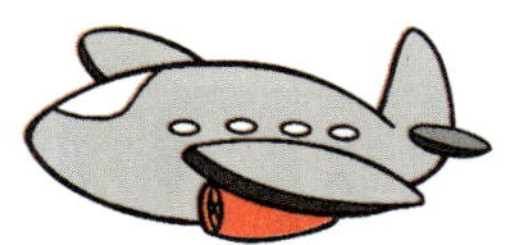 

Write the letter. Circle the picture with the same **ending** sound.

1.    

2.    

3.  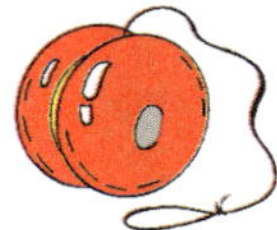  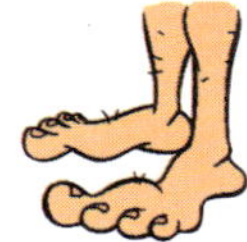

4.    

5.    

Phonics Skills

Circle the word that tells about the picture.

1. 

man
mat

2. 
cap
can

3. 
fat
fan

4. 
pan
pat

5. 
cat
can

6. 
van
vat

7. 
rat
ran

8. 
bat
ban

9. 
mat
man

10. 
fan
fat

Who can jump?
Yakko can jump.
Yakko can jump in.
Yakko can't jump out.
Dot can sit and ride.

Finish the sentence. Draw a line under the word.

1. The boys go ____.
   in   out

2. ____ rides in the park.
   Dot   You

3. The boys ____ and fish.
   jump   sit

4. ____ can fish now?
   Too   Who

5. The fish jump ____.
   out   in

6. Now the fish jump ____.
   out   in

COMPREHENSION

in out sit Who

Look at the picture. Choose the word to finish the sentence. Write the word.

1. Who can go to the park?

2. I can't go ______.

3. I can sit ______ the house.

4. I can ______ and look.

5. ______ rides to the park?

Draw a line under the answer. Write the word.

1. Who rides up to the ____?
   fish   house

   house

2. ____ rides to the house.
   Now   Dot

3. Go in and sit ____.
   down   out

4. Sit down and you can ____.
   jump   see

5. You can't ____ in the house.
   ride   fish

6. You can go ____ and ride.
   in   out

Read the story.

Girls ride in the park.
Boys ride in the park, too.
The boys and girls see a friend.

She can ride.
She can sit and fish.
Can the boys and girls fish?

Finish the sentence. Draw a line under the word.

1. Girls ____.
   sit   ride

2. Boys ride, ____.
   too   out

3. Girls ride in the ____.
   house   park

4. ____ and girls see a friend.
   Fish   Boys

5. She can ____.
   ride   jump

6. She can ____.
   jump   fish

7. Can the ____ fish?
   boys   man

8. Can the girls ____?
   fish   ride

PHONICS SKILLS

Write the letter. Circle the picture with the same **ending** sound.

1. 

2. 

3. dog

4. 

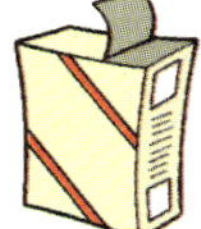

5. dog

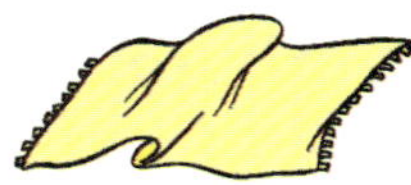

PHONICS SKILLS

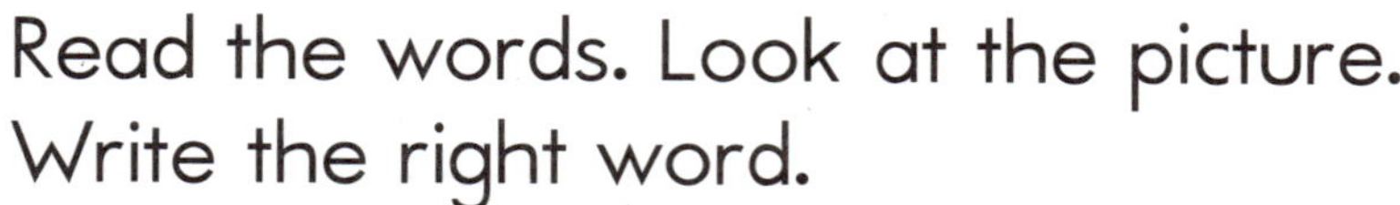

Read the words. Look at the picture.
Write the right word.

1. girl
   girls

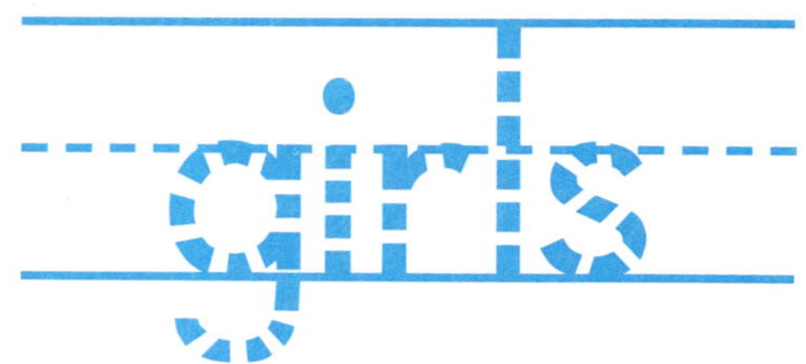

The ______ ride.

2. boy
   boys

The ______ rides, too.

3. park
   parks

Ride to the ______.

4. boy
   boys

The ______ can fish.

Study Skills

a b c d e f g h i j k l m

n o p q r s t u v w x y z

Write the letters in the right order.

1. h g i — g h i

2. 

3. c e d

4. s t r

5. v u w

Comprehension

See the dog.
The dog rides out of the park.
The big man rides out of the park.
The little man rides, too.

Read the sentence.
Circle the picture that goes with the sentence.

1. The dog can sit.

2. The little dog rides.

3. The big dog can jump.

4. Go out of the house.

COMPREHENSION

Draw a line under the sentence that tells about the picture.

1. 

A fish jumps out.
A dog jumps out.

2. 

Sit down, little fish.
Sit down, little dogs.

3. 

See the dog sit down.
See the dog jump up.

4. 

The dogs go out of the house.
The boys go into the house.

5. 

The little girls can ride.
The little boys can ride.

COMPREHENSION

Draw a line under the answer. Write the word.

1. The girls go into the ____.
   block park

2. The ____ go, too.
   dogs fish

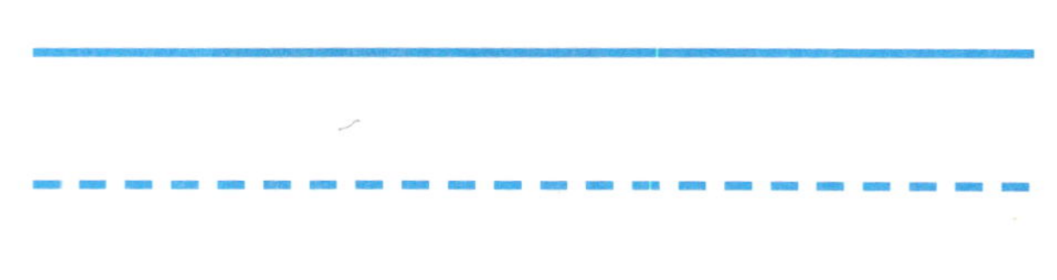

3. The ____ jump up and down.
   boys man

4. The dogs ____, too.
   fish jump

5. The dogs go ____ the house.
   up into

6. Now the girls can ____.
   jumps ride

Comprehension

Circle the picture that goes with the story.

1. You see stairs in a house.
   You go up and down stairs.

2. You see a pond in a park.
   You can fish in a pond.

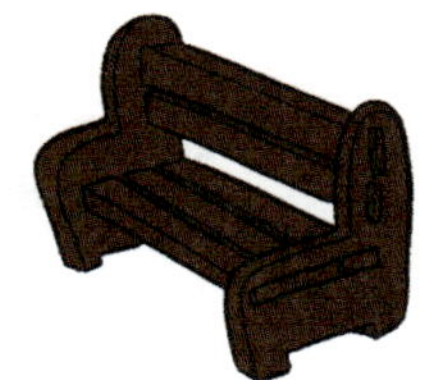

3. You can drive into a garage.
   You can drive out of a garage.

4. A kangaroo jumps and jumps.
   You can't ride on a kangaroo.

5. You see a door in a house.
   A door can't go up.

 PHONICS SKILLS

Write the letter. Circle the picture with the same **ending** sound.

1. 

2. 

3. 

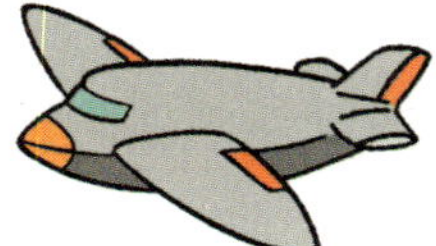

4. 

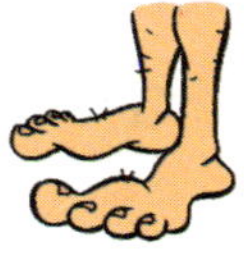

5. 

PHONICS SKILLS

coat

jar

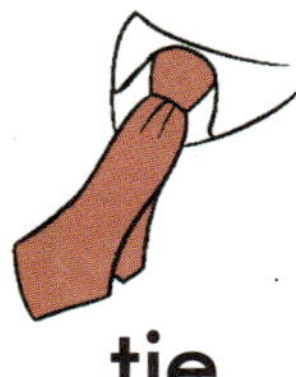
tie

rug

Name the picture. Circle the letter with the same **beginning** sound.

1. 
c j t r

2. 
j c r t

3. 
t r c j

4. 
r t j c

5. 
j c r t

6. 
t r c j

7. 
r t j c

8. 
c j t r

9. 
t r c j

10. 
r t j c

11. 
c j t r

12. 
j c r t

13. 
r t j c

14. 
t r c j

15. 
j c r t

16. c j t r

COMPREHENSION

Boys and girls like the park.
Why do the boys and girls sit?
The boys and girls read.
Does the man read, too?

Read the sentence.
Circle the picture that goes with the sentence.

1. The girls read.

2. Why can't he read?

3. Why does he ride?

4. He likes to read, too.

COMPREHENSION

does	read	why	boy

Look at the picture. Choose the word to finish the sentence. Write the word.

1. The girls like to read.

2. Why ______ the boy read?

3. Can you see ______?

4. The ______ can ride now.

5. He can sit and ______.

COMPREHENSION

Draw a line under the answer. Write the word.

1. Boys and girls like the _____ .
   house park

   park

2. The big dog _____ .
   reads jumps

3. Boys and girls _____ .
   but read

4. That boy can _____ .
   ride out

5. Boys and _____ like the park.
   fish girls

6. Can you see _____ ?
   does why

COMPREHENSION

Look at the pictures. Write the right number for each sentence.

A.

_____ Can the dog jump up?

_____ The dog is out.

_____ The dog jumps down.

B.

_____ He lands in the park.

_____ Can the wolf jump?

_____ The wolf jumps down.

PHONICS SKILLS

 lamp	 nest	 sock	 dog

Name the picture. Circle the letter with the same **beginning** sound.

1.  n l d s	2.  l n s d	3.  s d l n	4.  d s n l
5.  s d l n	6.  n l d s	7. 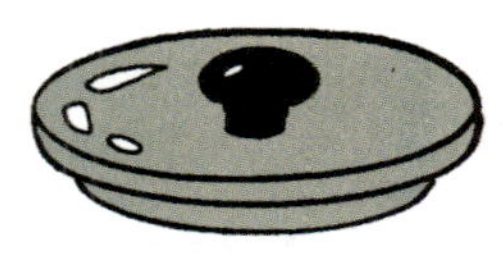 d s n l	8. 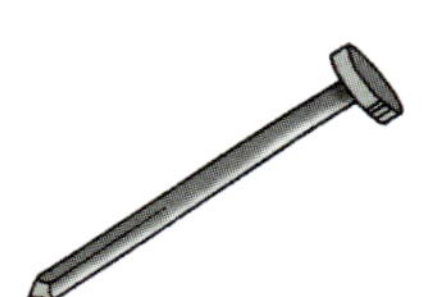 l n s d
9.  d s n l	10.  s d l n	11.  l n s d	12.  n l d s
13.  d s n l	14.  s d l n	15.  n l d s	16.  l n s d

PHONICS SKILLS

bed

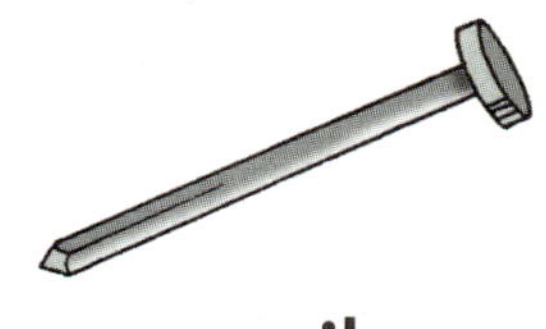
nail

ball

Write the letter. Circle the picture with the same **ending** sound.

1. 

2. 

  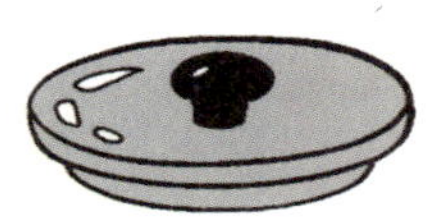

3. 

4. 

5. 

LANGUAGE SKILLS

Circle the word. Write it on the line.
Finish the sentence.

1. Little
   little
   Little dogs jump .

2. big
   Big
   dogs sit down ____

3. dogs
   Dogs
   can see ____

4. Girls
   girls
   go to the park ____

5. the
   The
   man rides ____

6. Now
   now
   you can fish ____

COMPREHENSION

I see <u>one</u> <u>word</u>.
That <u>is</u> a little word.
I <u>call</u> to the boys.
Can the boys read the word?

Read the sentence. Circle the picture that goes with the sentence.

1. Who is that?

2. The girls call out.

3. Read the word.

4. Can you see one fish?

COMPREHENSION

Draw a line under the sentence that tells about the picture.

1. 

Who is that man?
Who is that girl?

2. 

He calls his friend.
He likes fish.

3. 

The man jumps and jumps.
The boy sees one word.

4. 

A girl rides to the man.
The man rides to the girl.

5. 

The girl likes one little dog.
The girl rides and rides.

COMPREHENSION

Draw a line under the answer. Write the word.

1. The girl calls and ____ .
   calls   likes
   calls

2. Who is ____ ?
   Dot   girl

3. Dot is a ____ .
   girl   boy

4. The girl likes to ____ .
   can   ride

5. Dot likes to ____ .
   down   jump

6. Dot and the ____ jump.
   boy   you

Read the story.

The boy and girl ride to the park.
The girl and boy like to fish.
A big fish jumps up.
The girl can see the fish.
The boy can see the fish, too.
The boy and girl ride out of the park.
The fish rides, too.

Put the sentences in order.
Write the numbers 1, 2, 3, and 4.

_____ A big fish jumps up.

__1__ The boy and girl ride to the park.

_____ The boy and girl ride out of the park.

_____ The boy and girl see the fish.

 man	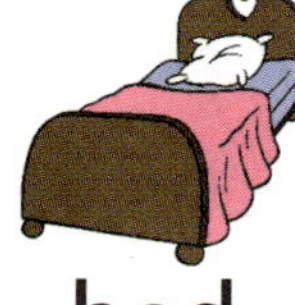 bed	 girl	 house

Name the picture. Circle the letter with the same **beginning** sound.

1.  g h m b	2. 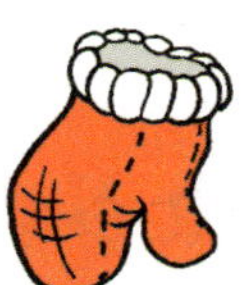 b m h g	3.  h g b m	4.  m b g h
5. 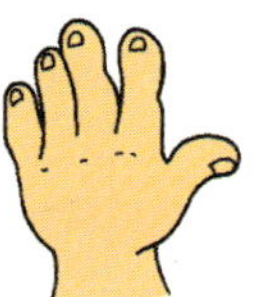 b m h g	6.  g h m b	7.  h g b m	8.  m b g h
9.  g h m b	10.  m b g h	11.  b m h g	12.  h g b m
13.  b m h g	14.  g h m b	15.  h g b m	16.  m b g h

STUDY SKILLS

Look at the picture. Circle the right clock.

1.    

2.    

3.    

4.    

COMPREHENSION

The mice are in the park.
The big mouse likes the hat.
The hats are down the hill.
The small mouse is sad.

Finish the sentence. Draw a line under the word.

1. Boys _____ in the park.
   are at can

2. The big boy is _____ .
   little sad up

3. Why is the boy _____ ?
   sad like hat

4. The dog is in the _____ .
   jumps hat ride

5. He rides down the _____ .
   hill hats house

6. Hats _____ down the hill.
   is are into

COMPREHENSION

are	hat	hill	sad	at	hats

Look at the picture. Choose the word to finish the sentence. Write the word.

1. The girls are ___at___ the park.
2. Why ______ the girls sad?
3. The ______ are down the hill.
4. A dog rides down the ______ .
5. The dog likes the ______ .
6. The big girl is ______ .

COMPREHENSION

Draw a line under the answer. Write the word.

1. The boy gives the man a _____ .
   park house hat
   hat

2. The big girl _____ to the boy.
   sits sees calls

3. The girl likes the _____ .
   that hat he

4. The boy and girl are _____ .
   sad at to

5. The man _____ down the hill.
   rides park reads

6. The boy and girl _____ the hats.
   run see call

COMPREHENSION

Which sentence tells about the picture?
Fill in the circle.

1.

ⓐ Boys and girls are at the park.
ⓑ The boys are at the park.
ⓒ The girls are at the park.

2.

ⓐ The little boy is sad.
ⓑ The boys are sad.
ⓒ The big boy is sad.

3.

ⓐ The hats go down the hill.
ⓑ The girls go down the hill.
ⓒ The hats go up the hill.

4.

ⓐ A dog is in the park.
ⓑ The dogs jump down the hill.
ⓒ The dogs ride down the hill.

PHONICS SKILLS

book

gas

kiss

Write the letter. Circle the picture with the same **ending** sound.

1. 

2. 

3. 

4. 

5. 

PHONICS SKILLS

 wagon	 key	 queen	 zipper

Name the picture. Circle the letter or letters with the same **beginning** sound.

1.  w k qu z	2.  z qu w k	3.  k z w qu	4.  qu z k w
5.  w qu k z	6.  qu k z w	7.  z w qu k	8.  k z w qu
9.  w k qu z	10.  z qu k w	11.  qu w k z	12.  qu k w z
13.  w qu z k	14.  k qu w z	15.  z k w qu	16.  qu z w k

STUDY SKILLS

CONTENTS

Find the story title above. Write the page number.

1. The Girl Rides Down the Hill 19
2. Little Hats and Big Hats . . . . ____
3. The Little Dog Jumps . . . . ____
4. The Sad Little Boy . . . . ____
5. At the Park . . . . ____
6. A Dog Can't Read . . . . ____

COMPREHENSION

Who likes the zoo?

She does.
She likes to walk.
She likes to look.
She likes the big bird.

Finish the sentence. Draw a line under the word.

1. Girls and boys _____ .
   walk ride run

2. _____ likes to run.
   Boy Man She

3. She is at the _____ .
   park zoo house

4. Girls see the _____ .
   dog bird girl

5. Boys _____ at the dog.
   like run look

6. See the boy _____ .
   walk ride jump

COMPREHENSION

bird	She	looks	walk	birds

Look at the picture. Choose the word to finish the sentence. Write the word.

1. She is a little girl.

2. The boys like the ________.

3. The ape ________ at the boys.

4. I see one little ________.

5. Can you ________ to the zoo?

COMPREHENSION

Draw a line under the answer. Write the word.

1. Ralph likes the ____ .
   big   zoo   call
   zoo

2. Kate likes to ____ and look.
   walk   read   out

3. Kate sees a ____ walk in.
   bird   fish   man

4. Kate likes to go up and ____ .
   hill   ride   go

5. Girls and boys look ____ now.
   little   see   jump

6. In the zoo is a little ____ .
   park   up   down

COMPREHENSION

Read each story. Fill in the circle by a name that could be a title for the story.

1. I like to go to the zoo.
   I like to walk.
   I like to look.
   I like to see the birds.

   (a) I Like the Zoo
   (b) I Like the Park
   (c) I Like to Look

2. She likes the birds.
   She likes little birds.
   She likes big birds.
   She likes to look.

   (a) She Likes to Read
   (b) She Likes Big Birds
   (c) She Likes the Birds

3. I like to walk.
   I walk to the park.
   I walk up the hill.
   I walk down the hill.
   I walk to the zoo.

   (a) I Walk to the Zoo
   (b) I Like to Walk
   (c) I Walk to the Park

4. You ride at the zoo.
   You can go up the hill.
   You can look down.
   Boys and girls look little.
   You can ride down.

   (a) Boys and Girls Look Little
   (b) A Ride at the Zoo
   (c) You Can Look Down

PHONICS SKILLS

cat	jar	ring	top

Name the picture. Circle the letter with the same **beginning** sound.

1.  j r c t	2.  t c r j	3.  c t r j	4.  t j c r
5.  t r c j	6.  r j t c	7.  t r c j	8.  r t j c
9.  j r c t	10.  t j c r	11.  c j t r	12.  r t c j
13.  j t r c	14.  j c t r	15. 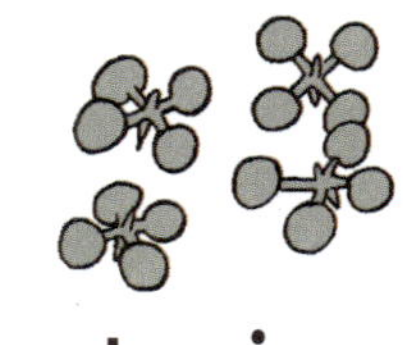 c t j r	16.  r j t c

PHONICS SKILLS

hen

bed

net

Choose the right word to finish the sentence and circle it. Write the word.

1. Nan fed the dog. — fed, red, bad

2. The ______ see the big dog. — men, man, pen

3. I see ______ little dogs. — tan, ten, den

4. I like the little ______. — pet, met, pat

5. I like to read in ______. — bed, bad, red

PHONICS SKILLS

bus

hook

hill

Write the letters. Circle the picture with the same **ending** sound.

Read the story.

The girl and the dog ride in the park.
The girl likes to look at the birds.
The dog likes to look at the fish.
The girl and the dog like the park.

1. Draw the park.
2. Draw the girl and the dog in the park.

Study Skills

a b c d e f g h i j k l m

n o p q r s t u v w x y z

Write the letters in the right order.

1. r p t

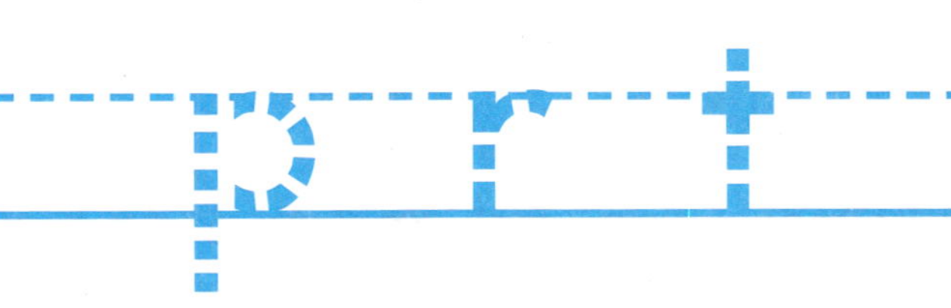

2. n o m

3. k f h

4. d b c

5. z s x

Answer Key

NAME
COMPREHENSION
Boys can fish.
Girls can fish.
Boys and girls can jump.
Can you fish now?

Read the sentence.
Circle the picture that goes with the sentence.

1. The girls can fish.
2. Now the boy can fish.
3. The boys can jump.
4. The girl can jump.

3

NAME
COMPREHENSION
jump can fish now you

Look at the picture. Choose the right word to finish the sentence. Write the word.

1. The girls fish.
2. Can you fish?
3. Now you can.
4. You can jump.
5. The boys jump.

4

NAME
COMPREHENSION
Draw a line under the answer.
Write the word.

1. The boy can ___. fish jump — fish
2. Now ___ can fish. boys you — you
3. The boy and girl ___. jump run — jump
4. ___ you can jump. Now Can — Now

5

NAME
COMPREHENSION
Read the story. Draw a line under the sentences that tell about the story.

A. The boys jump up and down.
The girls like to jump.
The girls see the boys.
Now the girls can jump.

1. The boys jump.
2. The man can jump.
3. The girls see the boys.
4. The girls can jump.

B. A man rides to the park.
The man can fish.
The boys like to fish.
The man and the boys fish.

1. The man rides.
2. The man likes to fish.
3. The girls fish.
4. The boys fish.

6

NAME
PHONICS SKILLS
man bed girl house

Name the picture. Circle the letter with the same **beginning** sound.

1. gate h g b m	2. bug g h m b	3. moon m b g h	4. hand b m h g
5. banana b m h g	6. hammer m b g h	7. gas h g b m	8. mop g h m b
9. helicopter g h m b	10. mitten h g b m	11. baby b m h g	12. garden m b g h
13. monkey h g b m	14. heart g h m b	15. guitar m b g h	16. bicycle b m h g

7

NAME
PHONICS SKILLS
hat pan

Write the letter. Circle the picture with the same **middle** sound.

1. hat — cup box bag
2. pan — cap socks belt
3. hat — pen flag book
4. pan — cat duck fish
5. hat — block truck bat

8

Answer Key

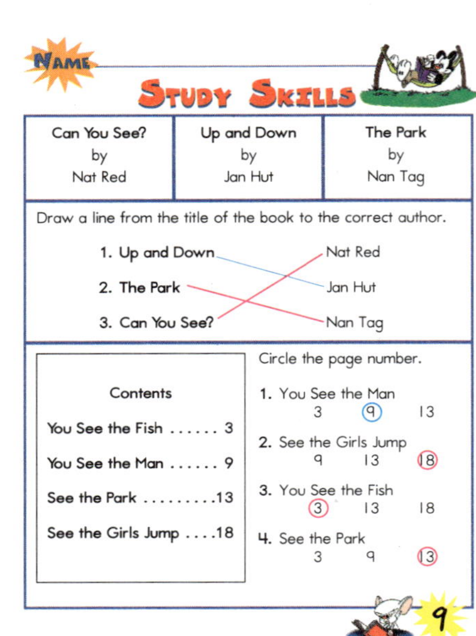
NAME

Study Skills

Can You See? by Nat Red	Up and Down by Jan Hut	The Park by Nan Tag

Draw a line from the title of the book to the correct author.

1. Up and Down — Nat Red
2. The Park — Jan Hut
3. Can You See? — Nan Tag

Contents

You See the Fish 3
You See the Man 9
See the Park 13
See the Girls Jump 18

Circle the page number.

1. You See the Man
   3 9 13
2. See the Girls Jump
   9 13 18
3. You See the Fish
   3 13 18
4. See the Park
   3 9 13

9

NAME

Comprehension

She can fish.
Can the boys fish?
Can I?
Now I can fish, too.

Read the sentence.
Circle the picture that goes with the sentence.

1. She can fish.
2. The girls fish.
3. I like to fish.
4. I like to jump, too.

10

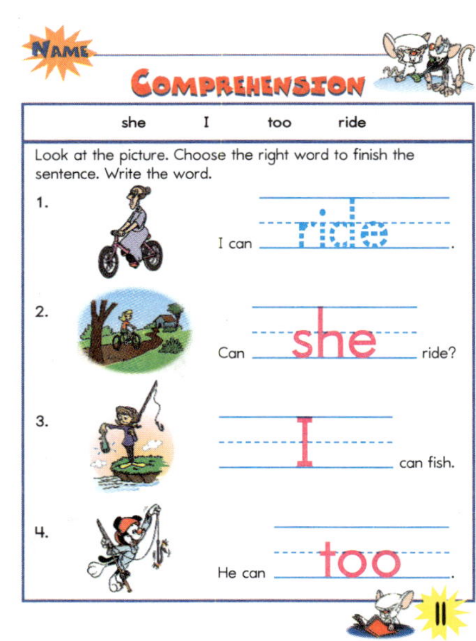
NAME

Comprehension

she I too ride

Look at the picture. Choose the right word to finish the sentence. Write the word.

1. I can ride.
2. Can she ride?
3. I can fish.
4. He can too.

11

NAME

Comprehension

Draw a line under the answer. Write the word.

1. He can see and ____.
   ride jump
   ride
2. Now I can ____, too.
   jump she
   jump
3. I see a ____.
   man you
   man
4. Can I ride ____?
   can down
   down
5. I ____ ride down.
   can see
   can
6. Now I can ride and ____.
   ride see
   see

12

NAME

Comprehension

Which sentence tells about the picture?
Fill in the circle.

1. ⓐ I like the man.
   ⓑ I like to ride.
   ⓒ I like to fish.
2. ⓐ Can you see the boys?
   ⓑ Can you see the fish?
   ⓒ Can you see the girls?
3. ⓐ The boys ride to the park.
   ⓑ The man rides to the park.
   ⓒ The girls ride to the park.
4. ⓐ He can jump.
   ⓑ The boys jump.
   ⓒ He can fish.

13

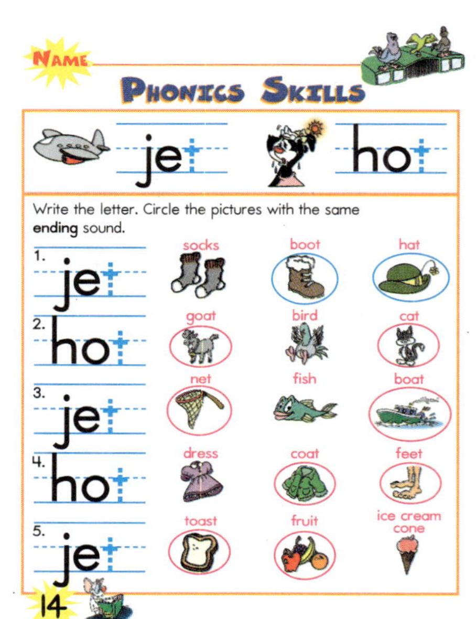
NAME

Phonics Skills

jet hot

Write the letter. Circle the pictures with the same **ending** sound.

1. jet — socks, boot, hat
2. hot — goat, bird, cat
3. jet — net, fish, boat
4. hot — dress, coat, feet
5. jet — toast, fruit, ice cream cone

14

ANSWER KEY

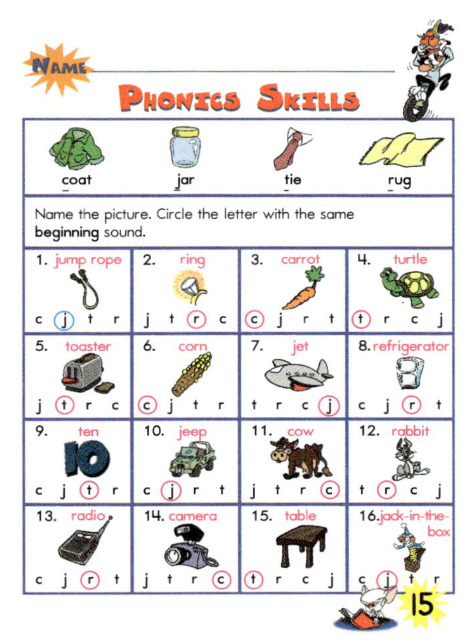

NAME

PHONICS SKILLS

coat jar tie rug

Name the picture. Circle the letter with the same **beginning** sound.

1. jump rope c j t r	2. ring j t r c	3. carrot c j r t	4. turtle t r c j
5. toaster j t r c	6. corn c j t r	7. jet t r c j	8. refrigerator c j r t
9. ten c j t r	10. jeep c j r t	11. cow j t r c	12. rabbit t r c j
13. radio c j r t	14. camera j t r c	15. table t r c j	16. jack-in-the-box c j t r

15

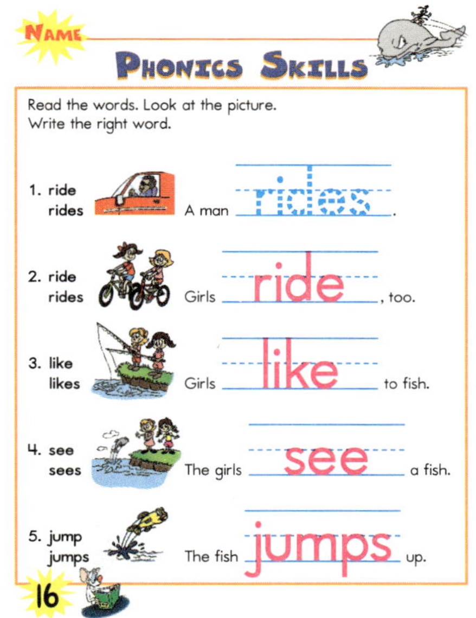

NAME

PHONICS SKILLS

Read the words. Look at the picture.
Write the right word.

1. ride / rides — A man rides.
2. ride / rides — Girls ride, too.
3. like / likes — Girls like to fish.
4. see / sees — The girls see a fish.
5. jump / jumps — The fish jumps up.

16

NAME

COMPREHENSION

Can you see the house?
You like that house.
Can you go in?
You can, but I can't.

Finish the sentence. Draw a line under the word.

1. See ___ man. You that
2. He ___ ride. can't can
3. I ride, ___ he can't. jump but
4. Can you see a ___? fish treehouse
5. I ride to the ___. house fish
6. I can ___ in. like go

17

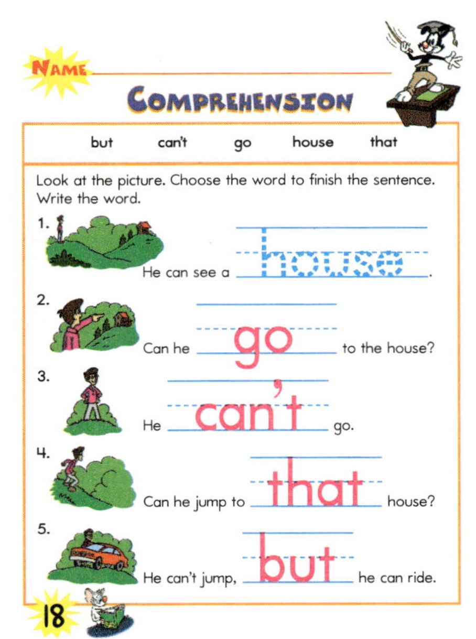

NAME

COMPREHENSION

but can't go house that

Look at the picture. Choose the word to finish the sentence.
Write the word.

1. He can see a house.
2. Can he go to the house?
3. He can't go.
4. Can he jump to that house?
5. He can't jump, but he can ride.

18

NAME

COMPREHENSION

Which sentence tells about the picture?
Fill in the circle.

1. ⓐ Jump on and off. ⓑ Jump on.
2. ⓐ You can go, too. ⓑ The man can go, too.
3. ⓐ Can the mice ride? ⓑ Can he and I ride?
4. ⓐ The boys can't go. ⓑ You can't go.
5. ⓐ I can go now. ⓑ I can't go.

19

NAME

PHONICS SKILLS

lamp nest sock dog

Name the picture. Circle the letter with the same **beginning** sound.

1. nurse l n s d	2. duck n l d s	3. seven s d l n	4. leaf d s n l
5. door n l d s	6. soap s d l n	7. doctor l n s d	8. lion d s n l
9. ladder s d l n	10. nine l n s d	11. doll d s n l	12. sink n l d s
13. desk d s n l	14. lock s d l n	15. squirrel n l d s	16. needle l n s d

20

Answer Key

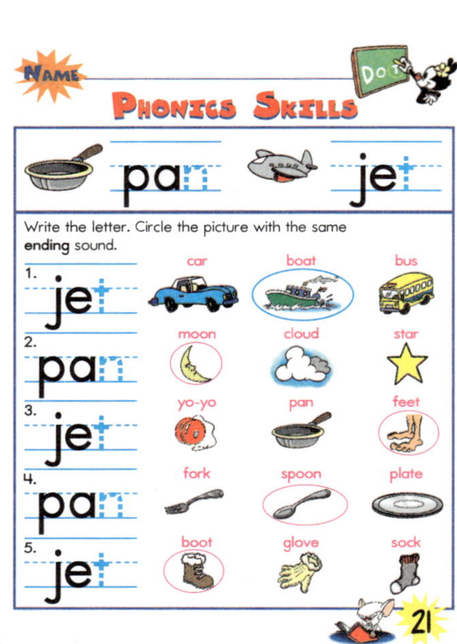
Name

Phonics Skills

pan jet

Write the letter. Circle the picture with the same **ending** sound.

1. jet — car, boat, bus
2. pan — moon, cloud, star
3. jet — yo-yo, pan, feet
4. pan — fork, spoon, plate
5. jet — boot, glove, sock

21

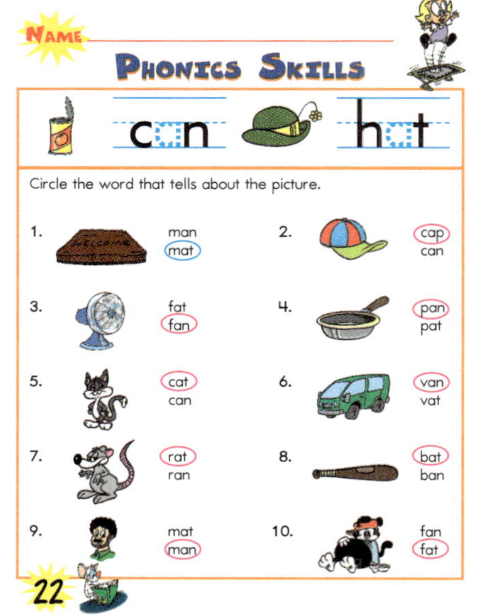
Name

Phonics Skills

can hat

Circle the word that tells about the picture.

1. man mat
2. cap can
3. fat fan
4. pan pat
5. cat can
6. van vat
7. rat ran
8. bat ban
9. mat man
10. fan fat

22

Name

Comprehension

Who can jump?
Yakko can jump.
Yakko can jump in.
Yakko can't jump out.
Dot can sit and ride.

Finish the sentence. Draw a line under the word.

1. The boys go ___. in out
2. ___ rides in the park. Dot You
3. The boys ___ and fish. jump sit
4. ___ can fish now? Too Who
5. The fish jump ___. out in
6. Now the fish jump ___. out in

23

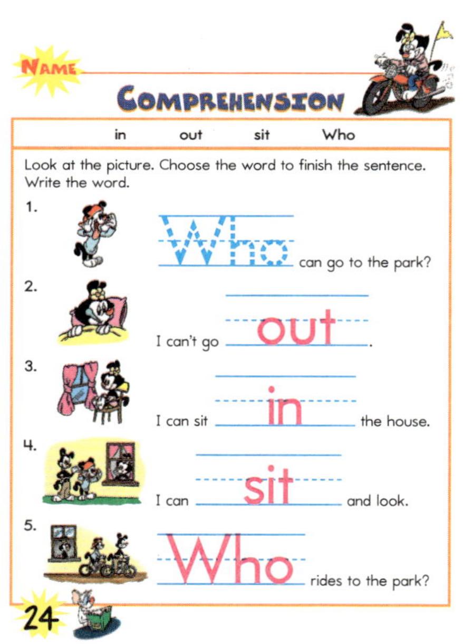
Name

Comprehension

in out sit Who

Look at the picture. Choose the word to finish the sentence. Write the word.

1. Who can go to the park?
2. I can't go out.
3. I can sit in the house.
4. I can sit and look.
5. Who rides to the park?

24

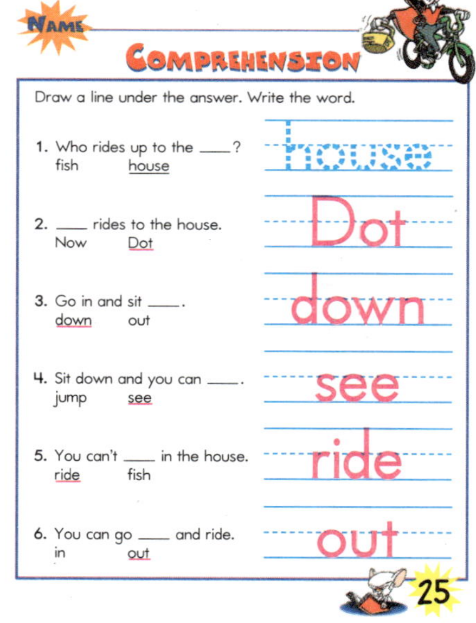
Name

Comprehension

Draw a line under the answer. Write the word.

1. Who rides up to the ___? fish house — house
2. ___ rides to the house. Now Dot — Dot
3. Go in and sit ___. down out — down
4. Sit down and you can ___. jump see — see
5. You can't ___ in the house. ride fish — ride
6. You can go ___ and ride. in out — out

25

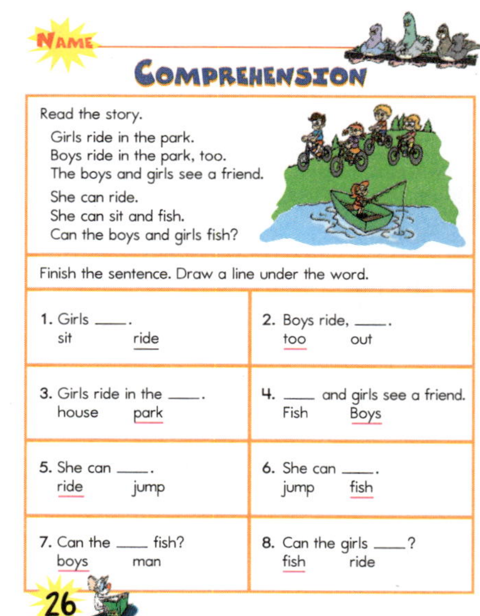
Name

Comprehension

Read the story.
Girls ride in the park.
Boys ride in the park, too.
The boys and girls see a friend.
She can ride.
She can sit and fish.
Can the boys and girls fish?

Finish the sentence. Draw a line under the word.

1. Girls ___. sit ride
2. Boys ride, ___. too out
3. Girls ride in the ___. house park
4. ___ and girls see a friend. Fish Boys
5. She can ___. ride jump
6. She can ___. jump fish
7. Can the ___ fish? boys man
8. Can the girls ___? fish ride

26

Answer Key

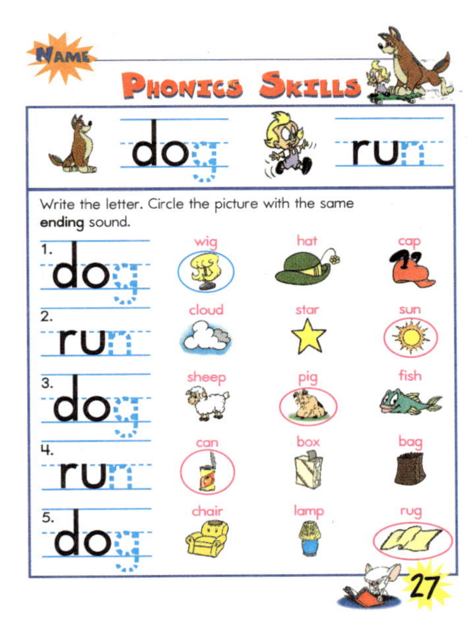
NAME

Phonics Skills

dog run

Write the letter. Circle the picture with the same **ending** sound.

1. dog — wig, hat, cap
2. run — cloud, star, sun
3. dog — sheep, pig, fish
4. run — can, box, bag
5. dog — chair, lamp, rug

27

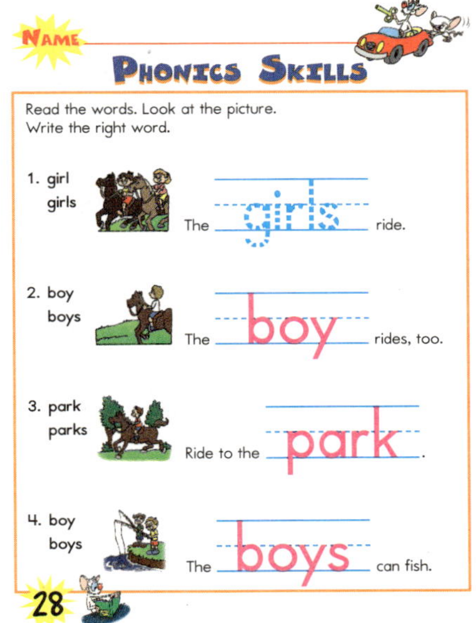
NAME

Phonics Skills

Read the words. Look at the picture.
Write the right word.

1. girl / girls — The girls ride.
2. boy / boys — The boy rides, too.
3. park / parks — Ride to the park.
4. boy / boys — The boys can fish.

28

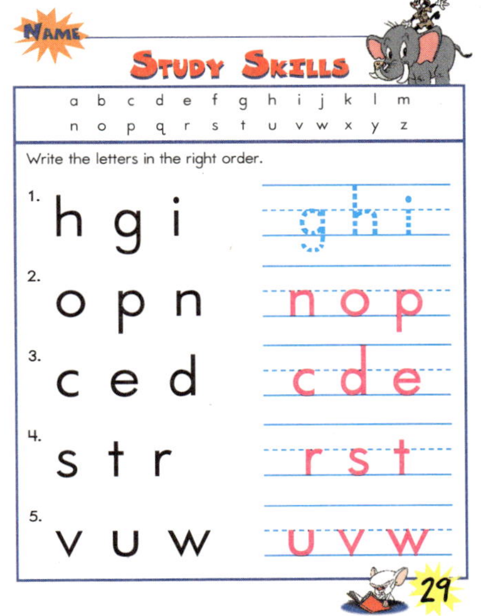
NAME

Study Skills

a b c d e f g h i j k l m
n o p q r s t u v w x y z

Write the letters in the right order.

1. h g i — g h i
2. o p n — n o p
3. c e d — c d e
4. s t r — r s t
5. v u w — u v w

29

NAME

Comprehension

See the dog.
The dog rides out of the park.
The big man rides out of the park.
The little man rides, too.

Read the sentence.
Circle the picture that goes with the sentence.

1. The dog can sit.
2. The little dog rides.
3. The big dog can jump.
4. Go out of the house.

30

NAME

Comprehension

Draw a line under the sentence that tells about the picture.

1. A fish jumps out.
   A dog jumps out.
2. Sit down, little fish.
   Sit down, little dogs.
3. See the dog sit down.
   See the dog jump up.
4. The dogs go out of the house.
   The boys go into the house.
5. The little girls can ride.
   The little boys can ride.

31

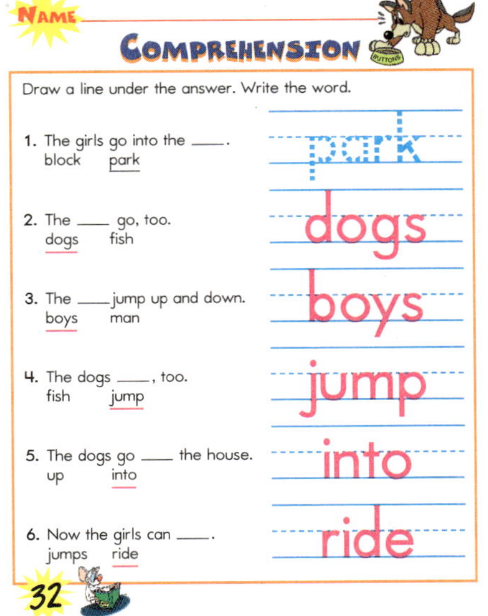
NAME

Comprehension

Draw a line under the answer. Write the word.

1. The girls go into the ___. block park — park
2. The ___ go, too. dogs fish — dogs
3. The ___ jump up and down. boys man — boys
4. The dogs ___, too. fish jump — jump
5. The dogs go ___ the house. up into — into
6. Now the girls can ___. jumps ride — ride

32

Answer Key

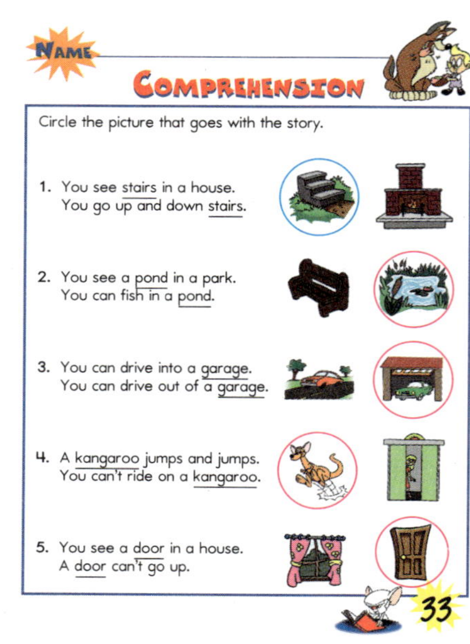

NAME

Comprehension

Circle the picture that goes with the story.

1. You see stairs in a house. You go up and down stairs.
2. You see a pond in a park. You can fish in a pond.
3. You can drive into a garage. You can drive out of a garage.
4. A kangaroo jumps and jumps. You can't ride on a kangaroo.
5. You see a door in a house. A door can't go up.

33

NAME

Phonics Skills

bed dog

Write the letter. Circle the picture with the same ending sound.

1. bed — book, bread, pen
2. dog — bear, cat, frog
3. bed — van, sled, jet
4. dog — leg, feet, lamp
5. bed — cloud, sun, moon

34

NAME

Phonics Skills

coat jar tie rug

Name the picture. Circle the letter with the same **beginning** sound.

1. jeep c j t r	2. rocket j c r t	3. table t r c j	4. car r t j c
5. jack-in-the-box j c r t	6. cow t r c j	7. rabbit r t j c	8. turtle c j t r
9. carrot t r c j	10. radio r t j c	11. jam c j t r	12. toaster j c r t
13. camera r t j c	14. typewriter t r c j	15. roof j c r t	16. jacks c j t r

35

NAME

Comprehension

Boys and girls like the park.
Why do the boys and girls sit?
The boys and girls read.
Does the man read, too?

Read the sentence.
Circle the picture that goes with the sentence.

1. The girls read.	2. Why can't he read?
3. Why does he ride?	4. He likes to read, too.

36

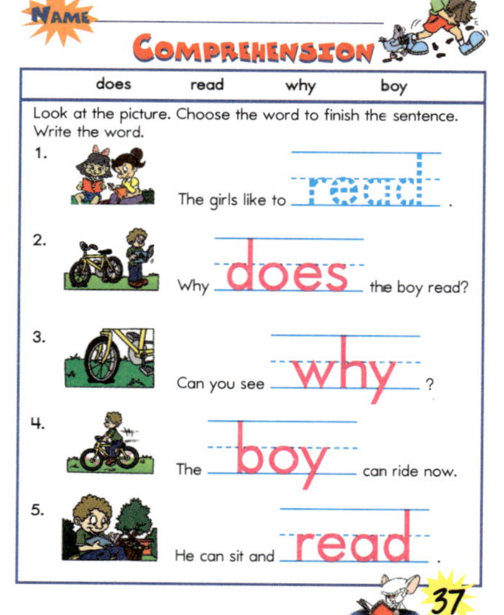

NAME

Comprehension

does	read	why	boy

Look at the picture. Choose the word to finish the sentence. Write the word.

1. The girls like to read.
2. Why does the boy read?
3. Can you see why?
4. The boy can ride now.
5. He can sit and read.

37

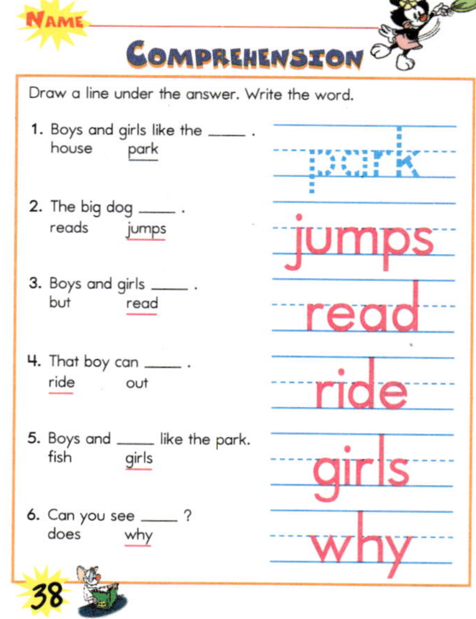

NAME

Comprehension

Draw a line under the answer. Write the word.

1. Boys and girls like the ____. house park — park
2. The big dog ____. reads jumps — jumps
3. Boys and girls ____. but read — read
4. That boy can ____. ride out — ride
5. Boys and ____ like the park. fish girls — girls
6. Can you see ____? does why — why

38

Answer Key

NAME

Comprehension

Look at the pictures. Write the right number for each sentence.

A.

2 Can the dog jump up?

3 The dog is out.

1 The dog jumps down.

B.

3 He lands in the park.

1 Can the wolf jump?

2 The wolf jumps down.

39

NAME

Phonics Skills

lamp nest sock dog

Name the picture. Circle the letter with the same **beginning** sound.

1. leg — n l d s
2. sink — l n s d
3. nuts — s d l n
4. deer — d s n l
5. six — s d l n
6. donkey — n l d s
7. lid — d s n l
8. nail — l n s d
9. dollar — d s n l
10. lemon — s d l n
11. newspaper — l n s d
12. sandwich — n l d s
13. ladder — d s n l
14. saw — s d l n
15. door — n l d s
16. napkin — l n s d

40

NAME

Phonics Skills

bed nail ball

Write the letter. Circle the picture with the same **ending** sound.

1. ball — well, doll, broom
2. bed — train, bread, lid
3. nail — seal, drum, pail
4. bed — cloud, sled, clock
5. ball — bell, boat, shell

41

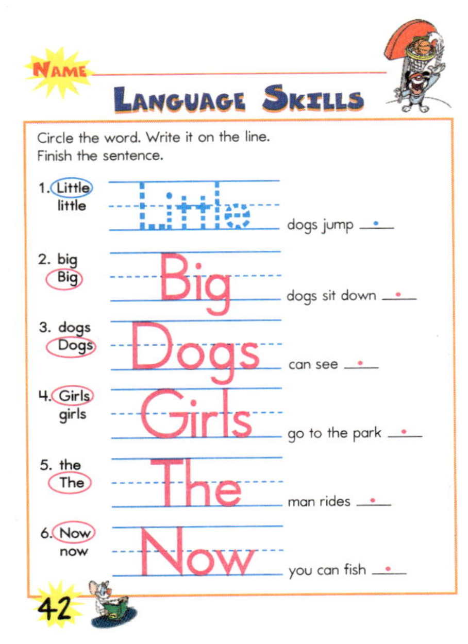
NAME

Language Skills

Circle the word. Write it on the line.
Finish the sentence.

1. Little / little — Little dogs jump.
2. big / Big — Big dogs sit down.
3. dogs / Dogs — Dogs can see.
4. Girls / girls — Girls go to the park.
5. the / The — The man rides.
6. Now / now — Now you can fish.

42

NAME

Comprehension

I see one word.
That is a little word.
I call to the boys.
Can the boys read the word?

Read the sentence. Circle the picture that goes with the sentence.

1. Who is that?
2. The girls call out.
3. Read the word.
4. Can you see one fish?

43

NAME

Comprehension

Draw a line under the sentence that tells about the picture.

1. Who is that man?
Who is that girl?
2. He calls his friend.
He likes fish.
3. The man jumps and jumps.
The boy sees one word.
4. A girl rides to the man.
The man rides to the girl.
5. The girl likes one little dog.
The girl rides and rides.

44

Answer Key

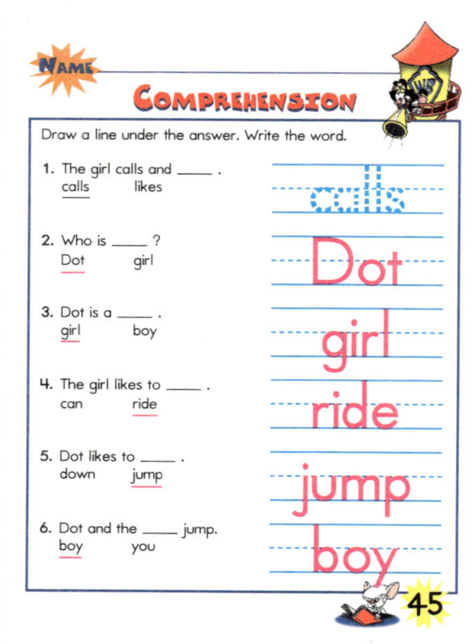

Name

Comprehension

Draw a line under the answer. Write the word.

1. The girl calls and ____ .
calls likes
calls

2. Who is ____ ?
Dot girl
Dot

3. Dot is a ____ .
girl boy
girl

4. The girl likes to ____ .
can ride
ride

5. Dot likes to ____ .
down jump
jump

6. Dot and the ____ jump.
boy you
boy

45

Name

Comprehension

Read the story.

The boy and girl ride to the park.
The girl and boy like to fish.
A big fish jumps up.
The girl can see the fish.
The boy can see the fish, too.
The boy and girl ride out of the park.
The fish rides, too.

Put the sentences in order.
Write the numbers 1, 2, 3, and 4.

2 A big fish jumps up.

1 The boy and girl ride to the park.

4 The boy and girl ride out of the park.

3 The boy and girl see the fish.

46

Name

Phonics Skills

man bed girl house

Name the picture. Circle the letter with the same **beginning** sound.

1. basketball	2. mitten	3. horse	4. gate
g h m (b)	b (m) h g	(h) g b m	m b (g) h
5. hand	**6. barn**	**7. game**	**8. money**
b m (h) g	g h m (b)	h (g) b m	(m) b g h
9. guitar	**10. hammer**	**11. merry-go-round**	**12. baby**
(g) h m b	m b g (h)	b (m) h g	h g (b) m
13. mixer	**14. garden**	**15. boy**	**16. ham**
b (m) h g	(g) h m b	h g (b) m	m b g (h)

47

Name

Study Skills

Look at the picture. Circle the right clock.

1.
2.
3.
4.

48

Name

Comprehension

The mice are in the park.
The big mouse likes the hat.
The hats are down the hill.
The small mouse is sad.

Finish the sentence. Draw a line under the word.

1. Boys ____ in the park.
are at can

2. The big boy is ____ .
little sad up

3. Why is the boy ____ ?
sad like hat

4. The dog is in the ____ .
jumps hat ride

5. He rides down the ____ .
hill hats house

6. Hats ____ down the hill.
is are into

49

Name

Comprehension

are hat hill sad at hats

Look at the picture. Choose the word to finish the sentence. Write the word.

1. The girls are at the park.

2. Why are the girls sad?

3. The hats are down the hill.

4. A dog rides down the hill.

5. The dog likes the hat.

6. The big girl is sad.

50

Answer Key

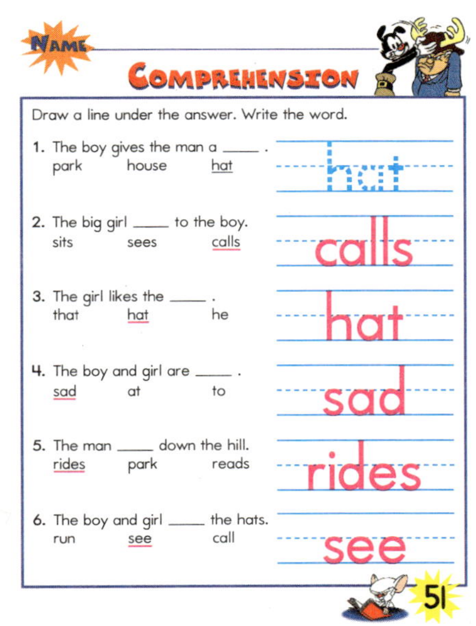

NAME

Comprehension

Draw a line under the answer. Write the word.

1. The boy gives the man a ____ .
   park house hat — **hat**
2. The big girl ____ to the boy.
   sits sees calls — **calls**
3. The girl likes the ____ .
   that hat he — **hat**
4. The boy and girl are ____ .
   sad at to — **sad**
5. The man ____ down the hill.
   rides park reads — **rides**
6. The boy and girl ____ the hats.
   run see call — **see**

51

NAME

Comprehension

Which sentence tells about the picture?
Fill in the circle.

1. (a) Boys and girls are at the park. (b) The boys are at the park. (c) The girls are at the park.
2. (a) The little boy is sad. (b) The boys are sad. (c) The big boy is sad.
3. (a) The hats go down the hill. (b) The girls go down the hill. (c) The hats go up the hill.
4. (a) A dog is in the park. (b) The dogs jump down the hill. (c) The dogs ride down the hill.

52

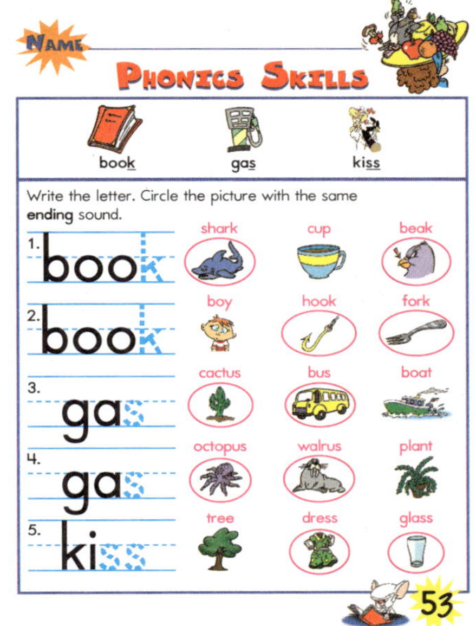

NAME

Phonics Skills

book gas kiss

Write the letter. Circle the picture with the same **ending** sound.

1. boo**k** — shark cup beak
2. boo**k** — boy hook fork
3. ga**s** — cactus bus boat
4. ga**s** — octopus walrus plant
5. ki**ss** — tree dress glass

53

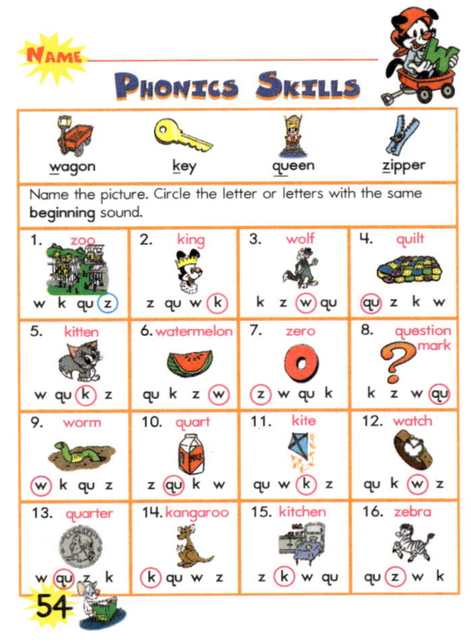

NAME

Phonics Skills

wagon key queen zipper

Name the picture. Circle the letter or letters with the same **beginning** sound.

1. zoo w k qu z	2. king z qu w k	3. wolf k z w qu	4. quilt qu z k w
5. kitten w qu k z	6. watermelon qu k z w	7. zero z w qu k	8. question mark k z w qu
9. worm w k qu z	10. quart z qu k w	11. kite qu w k z	12. watch qu k w z
13. quarter w qu z k	14. kangaroo k qu w z	15. kitchen z k w qu	16. zebra qu z w k

54

NAME

Study Skills

CONTENTS

Find the story title above. Write the page number.

1. The Girl Rides Down the Hill 19
2. Little Hats and Big Hats 2
3. The Little Dog Jumps 28
4. The Sad Little Boy 15
5. At the Park 7
6. A Dog Can't Read 24

55

NAME

Comprehension

Who likes the zoo?
She does.
She likes to walk.
She likes to look.
She likes the big bird.

Finish the sentence. Draw a line under the word.

1. Girls and boys ____ .
   walk ride run
2. ____ likes to run.
   Boy Man She
3. She is at the ____ .
   park zoo house
4. Girls see the ____ .
   dog bird girl
5. Boys ____ at the dog.
   like run look
6. See the boy ____ .
   walk ride jump

56

Answer Key

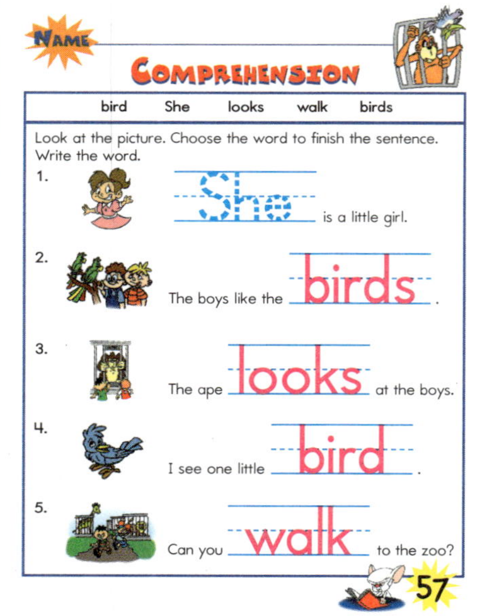

NAME

Comprehension

bird She looks walk birds

Look at the picture. Choose the word to finish the sentence. Write the word.

1. She is a little girl.
2. The boys like the birds.
3. The ape looks at the boys.
4. I see one little bird.
5. Can you walk to the zoo?

57

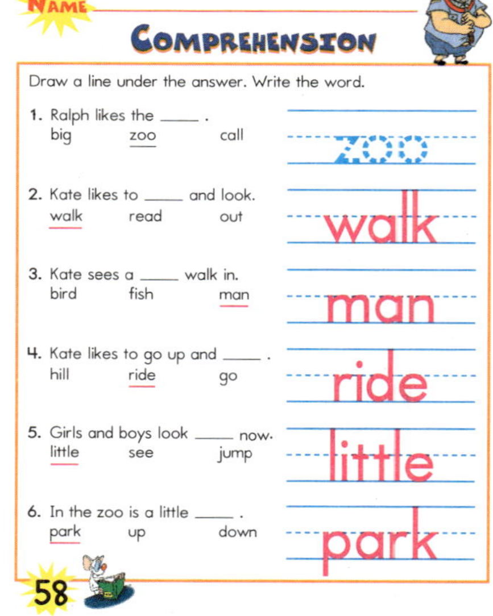

NAME

Comprehension

Draw a line under the answer. Write the word.

1. Ralph likes the ____ . big zoo call — zoo
2. Kate likes to ____ and look. walk read out — walk
3. Kate sees a ____ walk in. bird fish man — man
4. Kate likes to go up and ____ . hill ride go — ride
5. Girls and boys look ____ now. little see jump — little
6. In the zoo is a little ____ . park up down — park

58

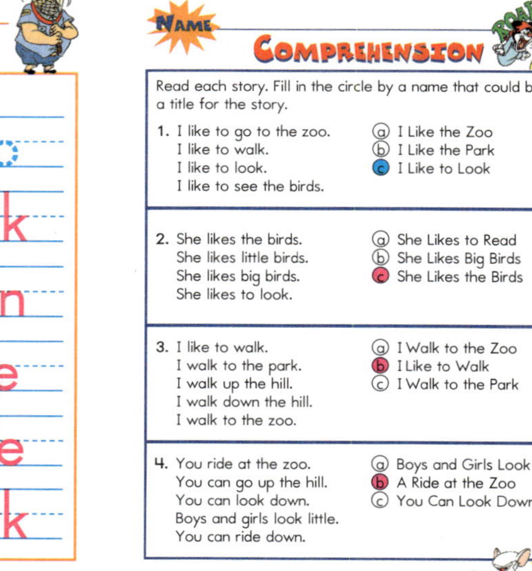

NAME

Comprehension

Read each story. Fill in the circle by a name that could be a title for the story.

1. I like to go to the zoo. I like to walk. I like to look. I like to see the birds.
   - ⓐ I Like the Zoo
   - ⓑ I Like the Park
   - ⓒ I Like to Look (filled)
2. She likes the birds. She likes little birds. She likes big birds. She likes to look.
   - ⓐ She Likes to Read
   - ⓑ She Likes Big Birds
   - ⓒ She Likes the Birds (filled)
3. I like to walk. I walk to the park. I walk up the hill. I walk down the hill. I walk to the zoo.
   - ⓐ I Walk to the Zoo
   - ⓑ I Like to Walk (filled)
   - ⓒ I Walk to the Park
4. You ride at the zoo. You can go up the hill. You can look down. Boys and girls look little. You can ride down.
   - ⓐ Boys and Girls Look Little
   - ⓑ A Ride at the Zoo (filled)
   - ⓒ You Can Look Down

59

NAME

Phonics Skills

cat jar ring top

Name the picture. Circle the letter with the same **beginning** sound.

1. rope: j (r) c t	2. table: (t) c r j	3. cake: (c) t r j	4. jeep: t (j) c r
5. cactus: t r (c) j	6. rabbit: (r) j t c	7. coat: t r (c) j	8. turtle: r (t) j c
9. two: j r c (t)	10. radio: t j c (r)	11. telephone: c j (t) r	12. cup: r t (c) j
13. jack-in-the-box: (j) t r c	14. cow: j (c) t r	15. jacks: c t (j) r	16. rake: (r) j t c

60

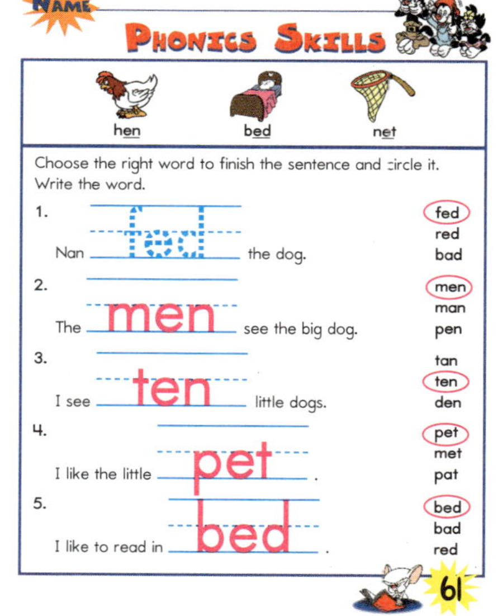

NAME

Phonics Skills

hen bed net

Choose the right word to finish the sentence and circle it. Write the word.

1. Nan fed the dog. (fed) red bad
2. The men see the big dog. (men) man pen
3. I see ten little dogs. tan (ten) den
4. I like the little pet. (pet) met pat
5. I like to read in bed. (bed) bad red

61

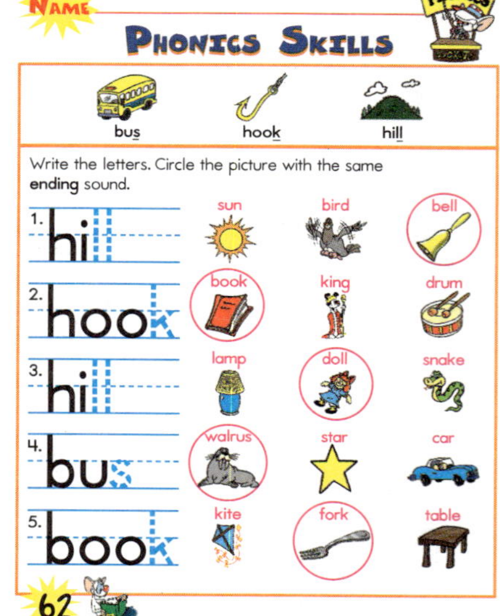

NAME

Phonics Skills

bus hook hill

Write the letters. Circle the picture with the same **ending** sound.

1. hill — sun, bird, (bell)
2. hook — (book), king, drum
3. hill — lamp, (doll), snake
4. bus — (walrus), star, car
5. book — kite, (fork), table

62

Answer Key

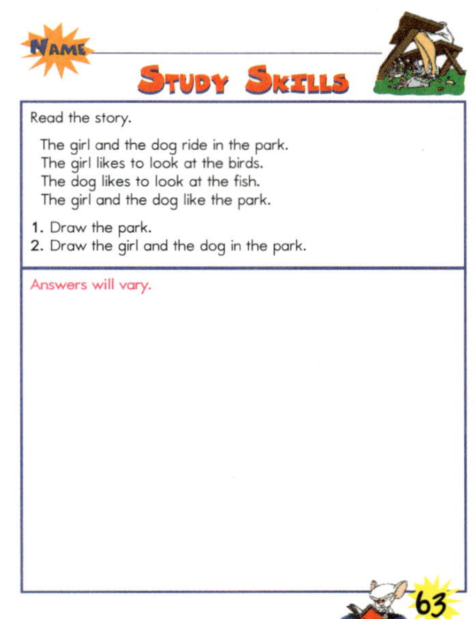
NAME
STUDY SKILLS
Read the story.
The girl and the dog ride in the park.
The girl likes to look at the birds.
The dog likes to look at the fish.
The girl and the dog like the park.
1. Draw the park.
2. Draw the girl and the dog in the park.
Answers will vary.
63

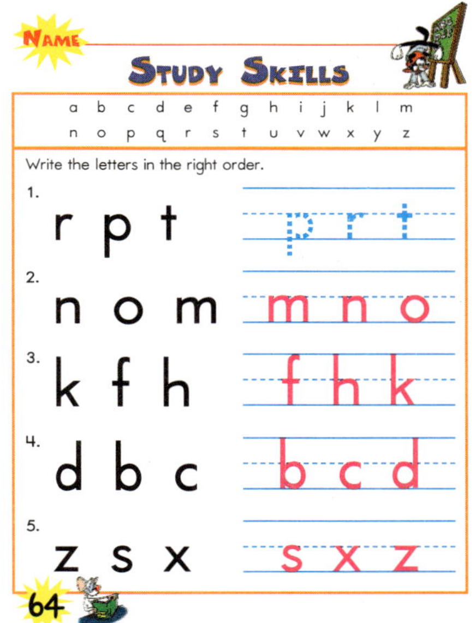
NAME
STUDY SKILLS
a b c d e f g h i j k l m
n o p q r s t u v w x y z
Write the letters in the right order.
1. r p t
p r t
2. n o m
m n o
3. k f h
f h k
4. d b c
b c d
5. z s x
s x z
64

Look for all of these entertaining and educational titles in

The McGraw-Hill Junior Academic™ Workbook Series

Toddler

My Colors Go 'Round	ISBN 1-57768-208-4	UPC 6-09746-45118-5
My 1, 2, 3's	ISBN 1-57768-218-1	UPC 6-09746-45128-4
My A, B, C's	ISBN 1-57768-228-9	UPC 6-09746-45138-3
My Ups and Downs	ISBN 1-57768-238-6	UPC 6-09746-45148-2

Preschool

MATH	ISBN 1-57768-209-2	UPC 6-09746-45119-2
READING	ISBN 1-57768-219-X	UPC 6-09746-45129-1
VOWEL SOUNDS	ISBN 1-57768-229-7	UPC 6-09746-45139-0
SOUND PATTERNS	ISBN 1-57768-239-4	UPC 6-09746-45149-9

Kindergarten

MATH	ISBN 1-57768-200-9	UPC 6-09746-45110-9
READING	ISBN 1-57768-210-6	UPC 6-09746-45120-8
PHONICS	ISBN 1-57768-220-3	UPC 6-09746-45130-7
THINKING SKILLS	ISBN 1-57768-230-0	UPC 6-09746-45140-6

Grade 1

MATH	ISBN 1-57768-201-7	UPC 6-09746-45111-6
READING	ISBN 1-57768-211-4	UPC 6-09746-45121-5
PHONICS	ISBN 1-57768-221-1	UPC 6-09746-45131-4
WORD BUILDERS	ISBN 1-57768-231-9	UPC 6-09746-45141-3

Grade 2

MATH	ISBN 1-57768-202-5	UPC 6-09746-45112-3
READING	ISBN 1-57768-212-2	UPC 6-09746-45122-2
PHONICS	ISBN 1-57768-222-X	UPC 6-09746-45132-1
WORD BUILDERS	ISBN 1-57768-232-7	UPC 6-09746-45142-0

Software titles available from

McGRAW-HILL HOME INTERACTIVE

The skills taught in school are now available at home! These titles are now available in retail stores and teacher supply stores everywhere. All titles meet school guidelines and are based on The McGraw-Hill Companies classroom software titles.

MATH GRADES 1 & 2

These math programs are a great way to teach and reinforce skills used in everyday situations. Fun, friendly characters need help with their math skills. Everyone's friend, Nubby the stubby pencil, will help kids master the math in the Numbers Quiz show. Foggy McHammer, a carpenter, needs some help building his playhouse so that all the boards will fit together! Julio Bambino's kitchen antics will surely burn his pastries if you don't help him set the clock timer correctly! We can't forget Turbo Tomato, a fruit with a passion for adventure, who needs help calculating his daredevil stunts.

Math Grades 1 & 2 use a tested, proven approach to reinforcing your child's math skills while keeping him or her intrigued with Nubby and his collection of crazy friends.

TITLE	ISBN	PRICE
Grade 1: Nubby's Quiz Show	1-57768-011-1	$14.95
Grade 2: Foggy McHammer's Treehouse	1-57768-012-X	$14.95

MISSION MASTERS™ MATH AND LANGUAGE ARTS

The Mission Masters™—Pauline, Rakeem, Mia, and T.J.—need your help. The Mission Masters™ are a team of young agents working for the Intelliforce Agency, a high-level cooperative whose goal is to maintain order on our rather unruly planet. From within the agency's top secret Command Control Center, the agency's central computer, M5, has detected a threat...and guess what—you're the agent assigned to the mission!

MISSION MASTERS™ MATH GRADES 3, 4 & 5

This series of exciting activities encourages young mathematicians to challenge themselves and their math skills to overcome the perils of villains and other planetary threats. Skills reinforced include: analyzing and solving real-world problems, estimation, measurements, geometry, whole numbers, fractions, graphs, and patterns.

TITLE	ISBN	PRICE
Grade 3: Mission Masters™ Defeat Dirty D!	1-57768-013-8	$19.95
Grade 4: Mission Masters™ Alien Encounter	1-57768-014-6	$19.95
Grade 5: Mission Masters™ Meet Mudflat Moe	1-57768-015-4	$19.95

MISSION MASTERS™ LANGUAGE ARTS GRADES 3, 4 & 5

This series invites children to apply their language skills to defeat unscrupulous characters and to overcome other earthly dangers. Skills reinforced include: language mechanics and usage, punctuation, spelling, vocabulary, reading comprehension, and creative writing.

TITLE	ISBN	PRICE
Grade 3: Mission Masters™ Freezing Frenzy	1-57768-023-5	$24.95
Grade 4: Mission Masters™ Network Nightmare	1-57768-024-3	$24.95
Grade 5: Mission Masters™ Mummy Mysteries	1-57768-025-1	$24.95

Look for these and other exciting software titles at a retail store near you.

All titles for Windows 3.1™, Windows '95™, and Macintosh™.

Visit us on the Internet at
www.mhhi.com

Offers a selection of workbooks to meet all your needs.

Look for all of these fine educational workbooks in the McGraw-Hill Learning Materials SPECTRUM Series. All workbooks meet school curriculum guidelines and correspond to The McGraw-Hill Companies classroom textbooks.

SPECTRUM SERIES

GEOGRAPHY

Full-color, three-part lessons strengthen geography knowledge and map reading skills. Focusing on five geographic themes including location, place, human/environmental interaction, movement, and regions. Over 150 pages. Glossary of geographical terms and answer key included.

TITLE	ISBN	PRICE
Grade 3, Communities	1-57768-153-3	$7.95
Grade 4, Regions	1-57768-154-1	$7.95
Grade 5, USA	1-57768-155-X	$7.95
Grade 6, World	1-57768-156-8	$7.95

MATH

Features easy-to-follow instructions that give students a clear path to success. This series has comprehensive coverage of the basic skills, helping children to master math fundamentals. Over 150 pages. Answer key included.

TITLE	ISBN	PRICE
Grade 1	1-57768-111-8	$6.95
Grade 2	1-57768-112-6	$6.95
Grade 3	1-57768-113-4	$6.95
Grade 4	1-57768-114-2	$6.95
Grade 5	1-57768-115-0	$6.95
Grade 6	1-57768-116-9	$6.95
Grade 7	1-57768-117-7	$6.95
Grade 8	1-57768-118-5	$6.95

PHONICS

Provides everything children need to build multiple skills in language. Focusing on phonics, structural analysis, and dictionary skills, this series also offers creative ideas for using phonics and word study skills in other language arts. Over 200 pages. Answer key included.

TITLE	ISBN	PRICE
Grade K	1-57768-120-7	$6.95
Grade 1	1-57768-121-5	$6.95
Grade 2	1-57768-122-3	$6.95
Grade 3	1-57768-123-1	$6.95
Grade 4	1-57768-124-X	$6.95
Grade 5	1-57768-125-8	$6.95
Grade 6	1-57768-126-6	$6.95

READING

This full-color series creates an enjoyable reading environment, even for below-average readers. Each book contains captivating content, colorful characters, and compelling illustrations, so children are eager to find out what happens next. Over 150 pages. Answer key included.

TITLE	ISBN	PRICE
Grade K	1-57768-130-4	$6.95
Grade 1	1-57768-131-2	$6.95
Grade 2	1-57768-132-0	$6.95
Grade 3	1-57768-133-9	$6.95
Grade 4	1-57768-134-7	$6.95
Grade 5	1-57768-135-5	$6.95
Grade 6	1-57768-136-3	$6.95

SPELLING

This full-color series links spelling to reading and writing and increases skills in words and meanings, consonant and vowel spellings, and proofreading practice. Over 200 pages. Speller dictionary and answer key included.

TITLE	ISBN	PRICE
Grade 1	1-57768-161-4	$7.95
Grade 2	1-57768-162-2	$7.95
Grade 3	1-57768-163-0	$7.95
Grade 4	1-57768-164-9	$7.95
Grade 5	1-57768-165-7	$7.95
Grade 6	1-57768-166-5	$7.95

WRITING

Lessons focus on creative and expository writing using clearly stated objectives and pre-writing exercises. Eight essential reading skills are applied. Activities include main idea, sequence, comparison, detail, fact and opinion, cause and effect, and making a point. Over 130 pages. Answer key included.

TITLE	ISBN	PRICE
Grade 1	1-57768-141-X	$6.95
Grade 2	1-57768-142-8	$6.95
Grade 3	1-57768-143-6	$6.95
Grade 4	1-57768-144-4	$6.95
Grade 5	1-57768-145-2	$6.95
Grade 6	1-57768-146-0	$6.95
Grade 7	1-57768-147-9	$6.95
Grade 8	1-57768-148-7	$6.95

TEST PREP from the Nation's #1 Testing Company

Prepares children to do their best on current editions of the five major standardized tests. Activities reinforce test-taking skills through examples, tips, practice, and timed exercises. Subjects include reading, math, and language. Over 150 pages. Answer key included.

TITLE	ISBN	PRICE
Grade 3	1-57768-103-7	$8.95
Grade 4	1-57768-104-5	$8.95
Grade 5	1-57768-105-3	$8.95
Grade 6	1-57768-106-1	$8.95
Grade 7	1-57768-107-X	$8.95
Grade 8	1-57768-108-8	$8.95

A McGraw • Hill/Warner Bros. Workbook

CERTIFICATE OF ACCOMPLISHMENT

THIS CERTIFIES THAT

HAS SUCCESSFULLY COMPLETED
THE JUNIOR ACADEMIC'S™

WORKBOOK.
CONGRATULATIONS AND THAT'S ALL FOLKS!

The McGraw·Hill Companies
PUBLISHER

Dot WAKKO Yakko
THE WARNERS–EDITORS-IN-CHIEF

RECEIVE THE McGRAW-HILL PARENT NEWSLETTER FREE!

Thank you for expressing interest in the successful education of your child. With the purchase of this workbook, we know that you are committed to your child's development and future success. We at *McGraw-Hill Learning Materials* would like to help you make a difference in the education of your child by offering a quarterly newsletter that provides current topics on education and activities that you and your child can work on together.

To receive a free copy of our newsletter, please provide us with the following information:

Name ______________________ **Store where book purchased** ______________________

Address ______________________ **Grade** ______________________

City ______________ **State** ____ **Zip** ______ **Title** ______________________

e-mail (if applicable): ______________________

The information that you provide will not be given, rented, or sold to any company.

Mail to:
Parent Newsletter
c/o McGraw-Hill Learning Materials
P.O. Box 400
Hilliard, OH 43026-0400

This offer is limited to residents of the United States and Canada and is only in effect for as long as the newletter is published.